Living
is
Giving

By the Same Author

SELECTED TO LIVE

TWIXT SOUL AND THE SPIRIT

Cover picture: The hills of Kilmartin, Argyllshire, Scotland

Living
is
Giving

by

JOHANNA-RUTH DOBSCHINER

Author of Selected to Live

LONDON

PICKERING & INGLIS LTD

1974

PICKERING & INGLIS LTD
29 LUDGATE HILL, LONDON EC4M 7BP
26 BOTHWELL STREET, GLASGOW G2 6PA

ISBN 0 7208 0302 0
Cat. No. 01/1210

Printed in Great Britain by Thomson Litho, East Kilbride, Scotland.

To all at home

who gave their time,

and to Rob and Sue who gave Barsloisnach

that these stories

might live.

Contents

Introduction

A book in your hand can become instructive, study material, an advisory service, it can bring comfort in your particular situation, or hilarious laughter . . . stimulating the respiratory system and toning your whole personality! This and much more is the purpose of our wide and varied field of literature.

With this book you have left the main line traffic and entered a siding.

You are holding in your grasp some very simple stories, day to day occurrences which YOU have created, and which unknown to you have brought rays of sunshine, happiness, thunderclouds of despair, marvel and astonishment, utter hopelessness or renewed courage . . .

to a fellow human being.

For obvious reasons, all identities have been changed, but you'll know the shoe which fits only you!

If you have not discovered *yourself* before you reach the end of these tales, at least you will have found a sure way either to chill, or to kill your fellow human beings—or to cheer and brighten their path.

J.R.D.

1   Mrs Munro of Buckie

Yes, Mrs Munro of Buckie, but it could just as easily have been Mrs Reid of Glasgow, Mr Galloway of Ayrshire, Paul Everett of Pennsylvania or Dean Dixon Rollit of Pittsburgh Cathedral.

The important point of the whole situation is that Mrs Munro of Buckie did what she knew she ought to do . . . She spoke ONE SENTENCE, one sentence only, and, like a stone thrown into a pool, it set ripples in motion, which spread in ever widening circles and once more the stimulus for positive action had been provided and . . . these stories of life reach *you*!

Mrs Munro of Buckie . . . spoke

Mrs Munro of Buckie . . . acted

Mrs Munro of Buckie . . . was the stimulus

You, who are reading these words, you, too, are that stimulus for another life!

You, too, affect the life of your fellow human beings!

With all my heart I wish to impress upon you that you are very, very important in this world!

You are capable of much more than you are able to comprehend. Believe in yourself, and trust that Invisible Power who made you.

That Power needs YOU!

Yield yourself for His purpose. Discover your true self and its potential. Become pliable clay in the hands of the Potter.

Trust that Power, meet that Potter, taste a new lease of life!

LIVE! GIVE!

2   From Turkey to Tissue

What could she do? There just wasn't a way out. It had been one hard struggle from day to day for months on end and now Christmas on top of it all.

If only Christmas could be Christmas for its own sake.

If only one was permitted to approach the Christ and worship Him in memory of that first day when His entry into this world changed the hope for mankind into a positive reality.

If only one could be still and express one's gratitude to the Father of us all, for Christ's birth—life—death and resurrection, culminating in the great gift of His Holy Spirit to those He had to leave behind.

The uniqueness of these great events, draws from one's inmost being a song of praise and dedication: 'Were the whole realm of nature mine, *That* were an offering far too small; Love so amazing so divine, Demands my soul, my life, my all'.

But no—Christmas means Turkey! Turkey and Christmas go hand in hand. She'd never get a turkey, not this year, but . . . she longed for *Christmas*!

Presents and other items needed attention—to so many the only means of assurance that they *do* matter, that *someone* cares. And the cards—for countless others a token that *they* are not forgotten, even if during the rest of the year no other communication reaches them.

Everything was organized. Everything had received attention, and so the days passed and nearer and nearer came Christmas Day.

No plans for a special meal, the Turkey now but a minor item of the 'impossible and unobtainable', but . . . *how* to tell the family?

Letters and cards galore arrived, providing decoration and setting the stage for the festive day. No one questioned the planning, preparation and presentation.

Should they?

Should she?

Among those letters was one with a difference:

Seasons Greetings. Yes, like so many, with sincere good wishes added, but *other* words made the letter tremble in her hands . . . an announcement of a Turkey to arrive in time for the festive meal!

Who would carve a turkey and serve a meal this Christmas like Rosemary!

Who would eat as thoughtfully and gratefully as Rosemary!

And none of the others knew about the fowl which might never have been!

Like the cruse of oil, there was enough until after New Year's day. Then, just the bones left, they were wrapped and disposed of . . . with reverence!

Once more the postman arrived at the house of wonder to deliver yet another even larger box, this time from far across the Atlantic. When all the wrappings had been removed by the entire family, big letters announced the intention of the sender: 'A PRESENT FOR YOU.' What *could* it be?

'Your heavenly Father knoweth that you have need of all those things!' Wonder of wonders, a *sign* of care for the fresh New year: from turkey to tissue indeed! Toilet paper, tissues, table-napkins, tea-napkins in abundance, towelling and all the small things one needs in the home, sent . . .

by her brother,

prompted by their heavenly Father,

to care for his sister . . . on time!

Matthew 6:33

3   Sharing

The beauties of creation, I read, were created for
    Your pleasure,
    yet, we use them for *our* pleasure . . .
You permit us to share Lord, YOUR creation!
    How beneficial and how generous!
Could you teach us to share ourselves, to let others
benefit from the fact that we ARE,
           that I *am*.
    All I have is Thine O Lord, a gift O Lord for
           Thee.
God doesn't want anything we have, except ourselves with the whole of our being, so that all nouns,
following our possessive pronoun, may share the
sanctified *self*
    with all those, whose lives touch ours.
           'Sharing',
a word so full of expression! Not 'giving', not
patronisingly parting with ourself, or what we own,
but allowing others to USE us and what is ours.
        Part of what we are!

★   ★   ★

Use us in our joys and use us in our sorrows,
use us when we're fit and use us when we're
    ailing . . .

★

The Lord was 'in use' all the time.

He shared Himself and all He was, even unto the death on the Cross.

And while you share this page with countless others, He shares Himself with you
as the ever present Holy Spirit.

*   *   *

'Teach me *how* to share *myself*, Lord!'

Luke 6:38

4 Coventry

Neighbours always remarked about the harmonious, happy family life of the Andorrens. One couldn't help noticing the unity which bound them together.

But then, one argued, no wonder it shows, haven't they everything to contribute to such a show! Health, strength, a fine home, a good job, well-mannered children, sound company . . . and many, many more things we outsiders don't know about.

He is a hard-working man, not much about, except at weekends, but she—well, one was continually bumping into her. Never short of time to chat here, to smile there, to phone a shut-in, to drop a note to any corner of the globe. She lived to the full and enjoyed her life.

The children were the jewels in their crown of thankfulness. Their phone hardly stopped ringing. There was chatter on the line, chatter while washing the dishes, chatter while walking their dog.

But once Rover was settled for the evening, the children retired to their respective rooms for homework, the house slowly died during the evening hours, and the same at weekends, especially on Sundays.

19

Silence reigned within those supposedly 'happy' walls.

He couldn't share his wife with that invisible, so-called Jesus Christ, and he expressed his disgust at her loyalty.

As for her, she couldn't reject her living, personal, *im*mortal Saviour, to please a mortal who wouldn't tolerate her devotion to a Creator to whom she owed her life.

Many an evening there were silent tears behind those drawn curtains and the closed storm door, above which always shone that bright light, illuminating the name-plate 'Sunshine Villa'.

Deuteronomy 6:4–7

5 PHS 775F

She's a beauty, yes, she is!

Clad in white, her lines display real elegance, real beauty!

So obliging, so co-operative, so desirous to move at her master's bidding. Yes, without him, she just won't budge, she stands and waits for orders, she rests!

Dormant, deep within her, there's life!
That little black heart of hers stimulates her whole being. Sometimes she feels lower than at other times, but a little boost from the choke and a firm pressure on that accelerator and soon she's her old self again.

Being tuned-in so perfectly to each other, this combination brought forth much fruit throughout the years. Everyone could see them together, everywhere, from early morn until late at night.

However, the day came when facts just HAD to be faced. She, like her master, was imperfect. One morning she just broke down completely. All zest gone, life ebbing fast: first one 'eye' would shine no longer and by ten o'clock her other 'eye' had darkened as well. Other motorists sought to encourage her by flashing *their* lights, but how *could* she wink back, she just wasn't able!

She needed expert attention and Campbell was determined to get it.

Imagine his surprise, when even the strength to let him out of the driver's seat was gone. The poor thing was unable to open her door. Inwardly, something had snapped! Now, wearily, he made his exit by another door, granting her repose for an hour or two.

What welcome awaited him on his return?

She looked at him, sadly, almost void of life in 'eye or heart'.
Front door still barred, he entered by the rear and calmly reviewed the controls, encouraging each in turn, engaging in the usual persuasion.

She would if she could,

but she can't, it's too bad!

How could she *give* what she just hadn't *got*!

O.K.—He understood!

An emergency call to the 'cardiac unit' of the local garage resulted in the arrival of an 'ambulance' in no time.

Dr Howie in charge of the investigation, examination and operation gave orders for a direct transfusion of power from the efficient 'ambulance unit'.

Campbell watched speechlessly as two tubes transmitted *that* which had been lacking in my 'girl'...LIFE!
Gladly now she continues to:

P —Proclaim

H—Him

S —Saviour

7 —to each

7 —and all, with

5 —five seats on the way to

F —Freedom.

Revelation 1:20

6 A Steam Pudding's Prerogative

A messy day. Slush, mist, drizzle and more to endure!

The fifty-eight bus jolted its way along the mushy road and came to a halt at the bus stop. People from one queue filed quickly into the vehicle, rushing for a seat to rest their tired, wet legs.

'Sorry, full up,' the conductor informed the last hopeful remnant of the queue. The fortunate few made their way to the remaining seats. There was still one left at the rear end of the bus.

A most elegant gentleman, dressed in executive style, complete with moustache, umbrella and brief-case, was heading for this haven of rest. His seatmate, however, who had only arrived a moment earlier, and being totally unaware of his intentions, had placed her gorgeous steam pudding beside her, while arranging her clothes and retrieving a purse from the full shopper at her feet.

Our immaculate gentleman, unaware of the delicious, but silent pudding on his seat, was rocketed on top of the poor thing by the eagerness of a punctual driver.

'Oh, no!' In desperation Mother Brown held up her hands: 'Sir, you're sitting on my steam pudding!'

Like lightning, he jumped from his seat, while Mum salvaged a flat sticky paper bag.

'Oh dear,' she exclaimed once more, energetically endeavouring to suppress her laughter, 'just like a Laurel and Hardy act!' Then rebuking herself for the comparison. 'He a Laurel or Hardy? Which?'

Both were soon united in uncontrollable and hearty laughter, infecting all in their immediate vicinity. Some had caught the cry of 'squashed steam pudding', others just saw the flat paper bag and were simply touched by this delightful couple of strangers.
In many a home that night, our poor, suffering steam pudding created an atmosphere of hearty laughter.

Thanks Mother Brown for holding an angry tongue!

Thank you, sir, for being such a sport!

A *messy* day with slush, mist and drizzle, became a *bright* day, because of this joy-ride.

Proverbs 15:13   Ecclesiastes 9:7

7 Mavine's Lamb-special!

Yes, Mavine really wanted to know about the lambs
in the meadows all around. She'd noticed their
happy faces, when they played
                                            and the sun was out!
I really had not watched them closely, and wasn't
aware of their smile,

    but since she told me,

      I promised I'd see

        their playfulness after my morning tea.

Yes, Mavine, you really were right; I saw them
myself today,

Ever so many, in every field,

      and sadness I saw not any.

How strange that they look like that e'en today

      although the sun does not shine . . .

Do you think, Mavine, these little ones know

      the story of water—turned—wine?

They even look happy in cold—windy—rain
they'll remember the previous day
when the sun played with them
and also will play
the following day again!

Oh, little lamb, teach *me* to smile
e'en when *my* sun does not shine,
when all my hopes just look like water . . .
teach me: *they'll* turn into wine.

John 2:3,5

John 1:29

8 The Divine Brainwave

Rain, hail, wind and snow,

Sorrow and sickness for high and low.

Trouble here, tragedy there,

All seems so bleak and all so bare.

> Life on the whole a struggle, a drag,.

> Nothing will ever just drop in my lap.

Evening, then morn—and another day,

And so it goes on and nothing seems gay . . .

> It doesn't make sense,

> There must be a clue . . .

> The *beauty* of nature!

> Yes, *that* rings true!

It didn't just happen, hey presto, that's that!

. . . There's order and beauty and peace! . . .

I stare and I wonder

I hope and I . . . pray

with some longing and yet in a half-hearted way.

Oh-make-me-aware-that-You-care . . .

★   ★   ★

There isn't a moment He does not care,

He's longing to touch your heart.

He made and sustains you,

He fashioned this work of art.

★   ★   ★

If still you doubt a true Father's care, reflect on the
first Christmas Eve.

Reflect and be silent

in body and soul

while

spirit meets Spirit

of

TRUTH

Aware of a caring hitherto unknown, will unfold
itself within.

God incarnate

Jesus Christ

born today

to

YOU

* * *

A brainwave? 'Twas careful and minute planning
for centuries, until that moment in time, when The
invisible Godhead, The creator of the Universe,
expressed Himself in a realistic and understandable
manner through

The Christ Child

born in

Bethlehem.

Isaiah 9 : 6

9 To be...
or not to be!

She wanted to know more about this Jesus. Rev. Quink knew Him and told anyone who wanted to hear about Him to go up those steps into that church building with the high tower and steeple.

There was no other way, she had to go up those steps. She had to! But all those people... Oh, they were a mixed bunch. Some smiled benevolently as she passed, time and time again. Others gave her a polite stare. She wasn't all *that* different! Why those looks? Her clothes were clean, perhaps not spot-on-fashion. She hadn't come to compete in a mannequin parade, she just wanted to hear Rev. Quink tell about her Friend, her dependable Saviour, Jesus.

Oh, there they were again, just like last Sunday; those six who were always together; a 'clique' you could call it. All fashion clothes, all pricey goods. Crumbs, what would they 'think' about her? What was hidden behind those kindly benevolent smiles? Shudder, oh shudder, no she wouldn't go in today. Rev. Quink had once said that you could have a tête-à-tête with Jesus Christ ANYWHERE...

Mary Magdalene walked smartly home to her single room while clinging to the promise 'Lo, I am with you alway'.

She feasted alone—and: received His peace!

Proverbs 29:23

L.G.—2

10 Twopence Worth

Her rhythmic breathing, her relaxed posture, just everything, indicated she was far, far away from the hustle and bustle up there in the Central Railway Station of the big city.

Down here in the ladies waiting room, it was so quiet and peaceful. There was comfort, flower arrangement and soft light, everything to induce rest or sleep, until someone approached with a noisy vacuum cleaner. She awoke and smiled.

'Had a good sleep?' I ventured.

'Did I snore?' she wanted to know.

Once her mind was at ease regarding this personal matter, she began to tell me about what had caused her this mental and physical exhaustion.

From the conversation which followed, I realized that she had spent more than seventy years on this earth and had just completed three weeks entertaining her cousin of seventy-eight and the husband of eighty-two. She had done all in her power to give them a good break and rest, and all had gone well until this morning. She had brought them to the station, but once they had left the taxi there were all those heavy cases to transfer to the train. Someone in uniform had told her that she could collect a self-service trolley; they were available right at the top end of that long, long platform. No job for her aged legs!

In the meantime, cousin and husband guarded the cases at the taxi rank. Our uniformed servant-of-the-public watched Grannie Smith make her long trek up the platform. Slowly, she pushed the squeaky trolley back to square one, whereupon the elderly trio made their way to the barrier.

It surely wasn't her day! The next obstacle was waiting right there at the gate: 'Platform ticket, please'. She did not have one and the machines beside her, stated coldly: 'EMPTY'.

'Ye need to get one down at the ticket office, sorry and all that.'

Almost pleadingly, Grannie had looked at the young lad, standing next to the speaker. Would he offer? Would he just run down for her? Just for one split second their eyes met, their thoughts seemed to merge, but 'youthful' looked the other way, busying himself all of a sudden with his nails.

'I'll be back soon,' she had told her cousin, and one more trek had begun. Queues, queues everywhere! At last she held her hard-earned twopenny ticket and slowly retraced her steps to Platform one.

That poor little twopenny ticket was punched right in the middle and then came to rest in Grannie's coat pocket.

Cousin Jane and Charlie left after a wonderful holiday, while Grannie Smith just spent one more little twopence to rest from the morning's ordeal.

No one to help, no one to assist, no one!

Yet, Grannie herself gives her own services free to serve the sick and 'elderly' with tea and comfort in one of the city's hospital tearooms.

She gives herself *free*, not earning a penny!

1 Corinthians 15:58

11 Spring

With a heavy heart and a sombre face he arose
once more to dress. Each day since early February
so bleak and dreary and joyless!

'How long', he pondered, 'must one endure this
endless monotony . . . when *will* we see the spring?

He saw when he made a point of looking, when
his longing to see was born, and he saw what
he'd longed to see all along, and hadn't seen before.

Children *now* wore cardigans and curtains
showed outside some doors.

A neighbour had started her spring-cleaning
spell:

in the park he noticed the goalposts: 'Wet Paint'

He longed . . . and he looked . . . and he saw . . . !

As he travelled in the bus to work, the morning
paper lay in his lap. He just longed and looked and
he saw such a lot this very first day of spring! He

actually parted with a spare smile for the man at the window seat, when he pointed out the many young lambs which hadn't been there last week. And a smile was born on that stranger's face and also on the lady behind, and soon all the others on that side of the bus, expressed 'spring' by actions so kind.

From the bus stop and right to the door of the shop, he whistled a brand new tune . . .

I heard him, I saw him, I know him so well, I can vouch . . . he's no more immune!

A day began with a fusty head, but a longing for 'something more', was rewarded with SPRING by 8.45 a.m. and inward sunshine galore!

Song of Solomon 2:11–12

12 Only a Moment

She passed his house but once a day, and ever so brief was this moment, but Henry was ready for well over an hour to catch just a glimpse and . . . wave.

Would she grant him this favour, perhaps today? Just a look, just a glimpse, just a wave? She'd done it once, some weeks ago, and that day developed such brilliance.

To a very old and lonely man, being shut-in all the time, the day can be brightened by anyone who will just lift their hand, just turn to smile.

He knows all who pass each hour of each day, the young ones en route to school, the salesmen, the bowlers, the shoppers and those who made it a golden rule, to turn and wave to the corner house . . . to grant just that second of time.

A second of time, it cheers the whole day for the one who must sit there alone . . . a second of time

    to spare a thought

      and a look

        and a movement of hand.

All but one sends this warmth, thought and smile
through the glass of that humble home . . . yet,
she'd seen him before and she knew he was there,
but she didn't quite know just *how* he would care.
She never thought to exert herself to share just a
bit of her charm; her dignity and thoughtless pride
did 'paralyse' her arm!

For Henry it set the pattern once more, for one
of those *im*perfect days. . . . If only she'd waved,
and 'why' did she not, yes 'why' did she not today!

For Henry, this simple thoughtless act had grown
to a mountain tall. 'She'd ignored him, she had,
now why had she, yes, why had she done just that?'

Psalm 138:6

41

13 Ever-Ready

The chief! Always in demand; regular hours an impossibility! His family had long ago given up the idea of a family dinner. During his early years, yes, one could be sure to have Yorkshire pudding with beef. Nowadays, it was beef . . . kept hot in the oven! Dad often ate his sustaining meals alone. Granted, the surrounding silence was beneficial, but it couldn't be called a life with a family atmosphere.

The Saturday before Easter he had left instructions at the infirmary: 'In an emergency, call my deputy.' This was to be a *family* Saturday, part of the youngsters holiday weekend.

Casual suit on, well camouflaged, he set out in his car to pick up a few weekend surprises for the family.

Right before his very eyes, his free day was shattered!
A bus out of control had demolished an estate car. He saw people, he saw blood, he saw despair and confusion.

This was his vocation.

This was his privilege.

These were *his* people, like *all* humanity!
He was the Chief: he had the skill and knowledge
to relieve pain and speed recovery. He had only just
left his home, but . . . was back on duty!

The phone rang at his residence.

His daughter answered reluctantly.

'Sorry, darling, I'll be away for quite some time.
Don't expect me till around dinner tonight. Sorry,
dear, it was an accident . . .'

Matthew 10 : 39, 40, 42

14 Good Friday

Volumes have been written to describe and to explain what happened that day on Calvary, but it leaves me speechless!

I cannot go into detail about the Event which has been described in well-known sentences, yet whose effect, with positive results, has reached down through history and touched me too . . . , even further . . . beyond my known span of years!

Domie rescued me from the grip of the destructive enemy force during the last war. He went *into* a dangerous hell, to keep me *out*, and when finally the decision had to be made *who* would be crushed by its machinery, instead of betraying others and me, *he* remained in its grip, awaiting the inevitable, so that others might live.

And we live and drink—in this span of life, until the awareness dawns:

we *too* are in the grip of death, right in the midst of it all.

* While Domie died so that we might live

    and give to friend and foe

a taste of that undying love . . .

    we see Another One go!

Here we stand before that Cross which has become the life-giving infusion through the ages to count-less numbers from all nations. To *anyone*, for The Giver of Life is not a respector of persons. We are invited to come, to accept, to receive.

It is offered freely from the Father God, through the sacrifice of His *Expression* of love on Calvary's Cross.

1 A new heart, to replace the stony one.

2 The life blood: flowing, cleansing and covering our dead nature of sin.

3 The Bread of life, to nourish us until we reach *that* Life which He secured for us through *His* death.

* page 224 *Selected to Live*

Matthew 26:26–29

15 Easter

No, this isn't a story.

The very word 'Easter' is a Beginning, which *has* no end!

Nor will I 're-tell' here, what we know since our earliest days.

How can one 're-tell' THE moment of Life, which will *never* see death?

*   *   *

The Easter of: '3-days-after-Calvary', has pursued us throughout the centuries,

and while we are reading this. . . .

we are enveloped in E A S T E R!

*   *   *

Once Easter, always Easter!

*   *   *

The Babe of Bethlehem

The Jesus going-about-doing-good

The Christ of the Via Dolorosa

The Saviour on the Cross

The risen Lord outside the garden tomb. . . .

IS with us *NOW*

EASTER!

Not *then*, but *now* is what saves your soul

Not *then*, but *now* He can make you whole

Not just *then*, but *now* He is able to bless

Not *then*, but *now* we can assess

how He lives and acts in lives which are His, by positive decision to let Him live

in daily events,

in sorrow and joy . . .

Easter an event, which NONE can destroy!

John 20: 2,19   John 14:16–20

16 You can't buy it!

A bubbling, bright, breezy spring day, an inviting blue sea, a quiet shore, too early in the season yet to be swamped by hurrying and scurrying humanity and the almost lifeless bodies of sun-tan seekers.

From the station platform I could see it all . . . the panorama before me and behind me, the trees, the hills, the grazing cattle, so unconcerned strolling from snack to meal, to banquet—above, the familiar blue sky, the occasional bird in flight . . . here, then gone again . . .

But most impressive of all: the silence!
For a time, I, the only passenger-to-be, refreshed myself from the view all around.

From just nowhere, a workman had come to join me.
His red-rimmed eyes looked out from an almost mischievious face. Oblivious to those tired or beer-soaked eyes, I was struck with his infectious enthusiasm. Whether it *was* due to beer or enthusiasm I would never discover as the train was due any minute now. But for those few minutes I was to be spellbound by his steady outburst from deep within: 'Saw you looking at the hills, aren't they great? You can't buy a sight like that, you can't! And look at those trees, look at the shading

48

of colours. Oh boy, oh boy, you can't buy anything like that, not with all the money in the world. To think it's all for our enjoyment, all without a penny admission fee. Isn't it just wonderful?'

On and on his adoration of the beauty around us continued. Daring to interrupt him, I ventured, 'These hills make me think of an old psalm full of good advice . . .' but breaking into my brief contribution, he was at it again: 'I will look up to the hills! From there comes my help! Aye, it's true,' he added.

I told him he was an inspiration.

'No me,' he retorted, 'I'm but a plain working man, a jobbing gardener, yet, I've all I want! Look around you, it's *ours*. Free! No lass, you can't but it, not for all the money in the world.'

And I had to board a train to the city.

Psalm 19:1   Psalm 24:1–2

17 The Wrong Bus?

There wasn't a shelter. Rain was battering down from heaven. Fortunately my bus was in sight and I ran for all I was worth.

I made it just in time, or had I? The driver slammed the door shut. The traffic lights at the corner convinced him with a staring red eye that he had to wait, yet he shook his head grimly at my pleading expression and posture. He wouldn't budge!

Subdued I stood waiting for the next bus which arrived sooner than I'd hoped for.

The conductor practically ushered me in, and one could be in no doubt as to the disposition of this servant of the public.

The weather was instantly forgotten together with my disgust over the previous unobliging, awkward driver, as I squeezed into my seat.

'Look at that,' the conductor announced from the front of the bus, 'look at that, she must have lost her purse—is she following us—was she a passenger?'

The driver slowed down and we all, with one accord, turned round and stared behind us through the back window.

'Ha, ha! look at her face now,' he continued, 'she's found it! Whatever it was,' he added in a lower pitch, finishing his lecture with his cheery chuckle, and . . . the passengers joined in.

We all watched him, in expectation of the next act. The bus drew to a halt at the next stop. The door opened, and as half a dozen passengers approached the steps, he held his hand up, crying out: 'Sorry folks, full-up!' Knowing this to be untrue, they stood stock-still for a moment, but as his other hand pulled the first one on to the platform, with grins on their faces, the others followed, filing into the empty seats.

'This is a mystery tour folks, we're doing a mystery tour!' And when one passenger held up her coin for the ticket, he was ready with yet another crack, 'Get your cheque-books ready, please.'

It was a cheerful load that jolted happily through these rain-drenched city streets, and when half of the passengers alighted before the great Motor Show, he let them leave with the cautious advice, 'Not more than one per family now; watch the taxman!'

We were enjoying our trip so thoroughly that I missed my stop. I hastily left my seat to watch the bus stop disappear around the corner. 'Oh dear, my stop,' I moaned. The driver, having heard my plea for help, slowed down, came to a halt, opened the door and let me out.

It *wasn't* the wrong bus! Countless people enjoyed not only a face-lift, but also a heart-lift . . . thanks to *that* bus crew!

Proverbs 17:22

18 That Fish

Between Easter and Whitsun, the programmes on television included a trailer of a brand new Disney film.

Meant for children, true, but one never fails to read that underlying moral for adults.

This time it was about a little boy, just craving for the moment when the conjurer, complete with top hat and wand, would transform him into a fish.

A fish, yes, a fish he had to be and nothing else would suffice!

The wand touched, the star glistened over and around him and a happy agile fish jumped into the lake!

Such a transformation, such delight, as he cruised through seaweed and plants and past the most sophisticated under-water creatures and fish. Our little nipper sported himself as an electric mermaid-like creature.

* * *

Why, I wondered, did the first Christians recognize each other by the secret sign of a fish? Did they long for the same mobility, the same freedom? I reflected over our Disney trailer, then light began to dawn.

Inquisitiveness, genuine enquiry or an unquenchable thirst, brings one to a kind of spiritual water which, when consumed, refreshes one's personality, outlook and standard of life in general. The thirsty one wouldn't have believed, if told what repercussions would follow the first mouthful. Indeed, one would never be the same again, after drinking from *that* water!

How many times had our little boy refreshed himself with water from the lake whenever desperately thirsty, before he took that plunge? The plunge into the mighty lake for which he'd asked again and again!

Water within, that indeed was necessary and so refreshing, but water everywhere would allow his entire being to perform with total freedom within the sphere so essential for his new existence.

A drink would never satisfy again! He would swim in this freedom always, confronting those new obstacles of the deep.

John 4:13–14   Luke 3:16   Acts 1:5, 8

19 Delightful!

The tea room was filled to capacity, the atmosphere was close.

No break this morning, no elevenses for the staff. They had to wait until after lunch. Short-staffed again!

It had been hectic since breakfast time. No sooner did someone leave their seat and it was taken by a newcomer.

My waitress looked harassed and exhausted, her rapid breathing betraying her constant rush this particular morning. The two extra seats at our table were occupied by a delightful young couple who had arranged to meet for lunch. The young man placed the order. 'Two poached eggs on toast and two coffees, please.'

On a small order pad, the items were noted and our harassed middle-aged waitress hurried once more to the hot kitchen, where she placed this last one, beside half a dozen other orders. She returned to the table after a very long time, with two cups of coffee in one hand and two plates with the toast and poached eggs in the other—at least for the time being. Gently, she placed one cup on the table . . . her hand began to shake . . . the second cup of coffee spilled just a little, but enough to make her lose control over the snacks in her left hand.

Slowly, but purposefully, the toast slid off the warm plate on to the lap of our young lady, and bounced ahead into her shopping basket . . . to meet the poached egg, which had got there first!

Coffee on coat, egg in basket, despondency in our waitress's face! Was it fury deep within our hungry couple! A call for the manageress?

Don't you believe it!

I overheard the young lady address the waitress while attempting to clean her new raincoat, 'It'll be all right, *I'll* use some warm water, while *you* get us some more lunch.'

A delightful personality!

2 Corinthians 1:4

20 It's All Right

It always is,

whenever one knocks at her door

and elaborately, awkwardly seeks to explain

why one has not called before.

    'It's all right!' How undemanding,

    countless lonely and elderly are,

    who seldom hear a human voice,

    who rarely ride in a car.

    Those who *suffer* alone and who *live* alone

    and who shop, cook and eat without health.

★   ★   ★

◀ *Photo: Copyright John H. Stone*

How undemanding and patient and kind!

What fragrance they scatter around!

They never complain,

they don't mention a pain,

for you're such a welcome sound.

When they hear you arrive their feast has begun

A memory they treasure for long . . .

While humdrum returns. Each twenty-four hours

increases their heart-throbbing yearnings . . .

Then when next you approach the door of her house

and you knock like the last time you came,

her gracious smile will *settle* you,

as she gratefully ushers you in.

Galatians 5:22

21 I Live,
Yet Not I . . .

'That's serious, that fellow needs a psychiatrist!'

Yet no other characteristic showed the need for immediate attention.

I had heard rumours about his mode of life and ways of expressing himself, and I left him, still pondering such an extraordinary way of speech.

He 'lives', that's pretty obvious, but 'yet not I' . . . who then does he make himself out to be? Perhaps he's some kind of mystic, some incarnation from a previous existence? A bit creepy! I discarded this thought at once. He was too strong a personality for that.

My interest now roused, I wondered if he would give me some of his valuable time for an interview.

He did.

It proved to be the most interesting morning of my professional life, so much so that the rest of the day was a loss, as far as my other work was concerned. It was amusing as well as searching and impressionable, for each time he asked whether I was sure he was 'really alive', with that sheepish innocent chuckle, I wondered what contradictory evidence he would produce with his next breath.

As the morning wore on—without the usual elevenses—I became more and more convinced that the rumours regarding this strange man were true.

He was certainly alive, and yet he was not an ordinary professional, someone else seemed indeed to be 'inside'. Would I call him a schizophrenic? Most definitely not. He recalled to me the immense value of that which *IS* 'life' in us. It's *THAT*, he explained, that is now under 'new management'. That bit which makes me 'tick', he repeated again and again. A Person! So, I live, yet not I, but One who GAVE His life for me, in order to live within.

Being lost for words, I took the sensible way out by saying . . . nothing!

He, too, felt there was no more to say.
Turning to the shelf behind his desk, he reached for a small paperback, handing it to me with the words: 'Here you'll find *why* I live, and what's *IN* living *FOR* giving.'

Glancing from book to speaker, then from his bright and honest eyes to the title, I read: The New Testament of our Lord and Saviour Jesus Christ.

I left him, convinced that no psychiatrist was needed, but a platform, a microphone and television cameras. The world must know, I insisted, that we are not involved with history, but with a present-day encounter with this Great One, who lives . . . to give!

Daily, year in year out, He looks for lives through which He may live . . . to give!

Galatians 2:20

22 To Chill—Kill or Stir—Move and Awaken!

Thank you for coming!

You came at your own expense, you undertook this long wearisome journey. You came, braving wind and weather, and you've accomplished your mission, we now see!

Your stay was brief, very brief, but you've made your impact; you've been the perfect defence lawyer for the younger generation.

You have tasted life, the life you chose deliberately with hundreds of thousands of others. You did it for them and for us. You became the expression of disillusioned youth and we bow our heads and confess to you and to all who stand beside and behind you, our united inadequacy and guilt. We were not the understanding, Christ-and-men loving creatures you expected us to be. We acknowledge the communication gap! We endeavour to bridge it!

Don't say 'too late now'!

Don't reject us!

Don't turn your back on us!

Turn to face us, meet us half-way. Come now, let us reason together and find a new way to walk side by side.

Was it post-war reaction? Once pressure was relieved, we let you and everyone go so free. This *past* . . . created your *present*! We stare at you and see . . .

The FUTURE is fresh, unspoiled, . . .

Act now . . . for YOUR children . . . or we'll all be lost.

Matthew 7:12; Joel 2:23–27

65

23 6.30 a.m.

How quietly the city rests during the early hours of morning. How undisturbed it is! One's own heart and mind ticks over that little bit more gently, that little bit more serenely.

'Tween five and six o'clock, all around seems to breathe peace!

It seems . . .

Yes, there's a Source of peace!

Come and sample it.

Come and lay the foundation for a day, unruffled by unexpected events.

*   *   *

A light in the paper shop!

They'd sell one, even so early . . .

Graham left the counter, came round, bending low among the bundles, selecting our choice. Then, straightening himself, he cheerily sold his paper.

Yes, *cheerily* he sold his paper, engaged in divine service, as the early customers select *this* shop to receive an encouraging stimulus for the day.

A sticker on his lapel urged me to 'Smile', for, as it said, 'God loves you!'

Fancy *that*, at six-thirty in the morning!
I caught my bus, but never scanned the paper.

Could it be true? what the sticker said.
That indeed was worth pondering. If true, it was worth more than all the news in today's paper.

'Smile, God loves you!'

Really? Do You? Just as I am today? Even after last night?

I dropped my paper and . . . smiling: BELIEVED!

John 3:16

24 Summer

Summer in all its glory is spreading throughout our land. All creation is so grand in colour, fragrance, scenery and power. . . . Strong winds in the cool of the evening, wide stretches of mist in the morn, and the dew is covering the valleys and all . . .

> without aid from science and technology!

It's a pity, but no one can take credit for this perfect creation, this perfect maintenance, no one can take it, but . . .

> we'd like to give it, oh God, unto Thee:

'Glory be to the Father, and to the Son, and to
   the Holy Ghost;
As it was in the beginning, is now and ever shall
   be;
world without
          end.'
               Amen!

★

I rest on the shore of Your ocean
And Your sun is providing the glow,
No centrally heated cabin
Could ever *this* comfort bestow

Photo: Copyright T. Parker ▶

Let me drink from the love of Your Presence
A refreshment fit for a king,
Oh, this summer sun is spreading right o'er
    me...
Hallelujah! I truly *must* sing...!

Luke 21:25–33

25 Chiropody

She had to leave school this year. She had passed her exams but she didn't have a definite aim. The careers' adviser had suggested that she should consider chiropody, but all she knew about that was an ingrowing toenail which some years before had thoroughly spoiled her holiday.

She a chiropodist! too funny for words! It sounded rather strange to spend all your working days cutting nails, removing corns and such like.

She was the only one in her class to consider such a job but she pursued the matter. The following year found her in training. Lectures, clinics, watching sessions, until eventually she managed to cut the nails of her entire family neatly and professionally.

For weeks during that first year, she would dream about feet. Feet of all sizes, shapes and description. Feet, feet, feet, and not all were carefully tended before they reached her hands.

Oh dear, working with feet, until some lovable suitor would snatch her up, propose, and then earn the bread and butter for them both. . . .

The future looked bleak until the summer holidays after her finals from college.

Walking along the promenade one sunny evening, her attention was attracted by a clear voice over a loudspeaker. 'He has no hands but our hands, no voice but our voice, no feet but our feet. Our entire body can be the vehicle for His will and purpose. Our body IS the temple in which He longs to live.'

Unobtrusively she joined the crowd which listened, while children continued to build sand castles and others enjoyed a game of football.

That night, not even the silence of that boarding house on the hillside overlooking the never silent sea could quieten her thoughts.

Her future unfolded gently within her mind.
Never before had she been confronted by the living Christ. During Sunday school lessons she had heard about Him from a book. She had sung about Him from another book. But today, today was different. She knew in an instant, that He is the same today as He was 2000 years ago. Not a bodily, visible Christ, but a risen ascended Christ, ascended in order to descend, descend right into any person who would welcome His divine Majesty.

'No hands, but our hands,

no voice, but our voice,

no feet, but our feet.'

In the small hours of the morning she left her bed and knelt reverently: 'Lord God Almighty, I'm a chiropodist; feet, only feet, are my responsibility. Lord, those feet belong to people. People with doubts and perplexities, joys and sorrows. People, most of whom surely never think about You. Lord,

▶

use my body as *your* temple, *your* headquarters, when I am on duty. Use my voice, and my hands, make them of use with the impulse of Your love.'

Since her holidays, scores of people entering her cubicle with sore feet, left to face the world with a spring in their step and new hope in their hearts.

1 Corinthians 6:19–20

26 To be a Widow,

to be bereft; it's as if one's very heart has been torn out, leaving you as a shell—so I am told.

Whenever such a one speaks, her conversation dwells on the past, on their wonderful days 'together', yet from there—the roads run into widely different fields of pasture.

'Why should it have happened to him? and then, the baffled cry of 'injustice being done in her situation'.

'He suffered so badly,' and then the story of his courage and endurance. Turning into oneself, turning *into* grief and developing that aloneness, seems the best way out to many who are bereaved.

Lives are torn asunder, lives are incomplete when separation comes. It's then we realize just how incomplete we really are and how the road we now have to tread, we tread alone!

But nothing, not even death, is able to separate those who serve the same Master, whose soul is made secure by the same Saviour.

Again and again this is being brought home to me by various people in different circumstances— although a separated-unit . . . they live to give! And what joy to meet such 'merry' widows.

'Merry' will never describe the radiance and peace which comes from such an often lonely life. I'd call it beauty! Beauty-plus which radiates *on* them, then through them from the origin of Life— from the life of Him whose separation is but for a while.

One thus bereaved revealed this beauty, and . . . made me glad!

Mrs Calderwood never saw anyone, for when you are past eighty, you need every scrap of concentration for the cleaning of your front porch and steps. Curlers in her thin, white hair, scrubbing with even motions of arms and body, the rhythm rang out over her front garden . . . to me . . . passing by just then:

> When He cometh, to take up His jewels,
> All His jewels, precious jewels,
> His loved and His own . . .
> Like the stars of the morning, His bright
> crown adorning,
> They shall shine in their beauty, bright gems
> in His crown.

* * *

This shining gem radiated during that morning hour . . .

an echo of life Eternal!

John 14:1–3

27 No Use?

Unshakable in her opinion! 'I'm not much good at 78. Have never been much use to anyone, really. In my young days, well, that was different, I did my best.'

She laughed an embarrassed—shy—chuckle, 'Charring that's what I can do. I can work, you know, I'm able as long as I keep going. No need for a washing machine, or any such nonsense. A bit of rubbing and scrubbing—that's what keeps my hands supple. The clothes will drip out in the yard and the good wind gives them a healthy fresh smell. Aye, I'll work in my house and toddle around, it keeps my knees from stiffening up.'

Wholesome meals are on each menu, empty tins are rarely found in Mum's dustbin. When her old man comes home from the bowling, there's always a warm room, a good cuppa and a cheery smile awaiting him.

They are all alone; the children, grown-up now, serve their fellow human beings in their respective spheres.

The daughter, a G.P. with a constantly growing practice, her generous personality a magnetic *must* for those in pain and bewilderment. The son, a motor mechanic—with a plus. He doesn't work for his wage alone, he works to repair a car with the same devotion as his sister seeks to repair sick bodies.

He knows what four sound wheels and a healthy engine can mean in terms of safety on the road. He's aware of the trust placed in him and discharges his duty with scrupulous care.

Even 'after' hours, he won't see an anxious motorist stuck. 'Overtime' doesn't enter his calculations. He lives—to give!

Mum has given LIFE to these two, nursed them devotedly through sickness and taught them the A, B, C of human relationships. Now they are able to face the stream of life and . . .

Mum still thinks, she's been of no use.

Proverbs 1 : 8–9

28 Service-Plus

The shell had blasted him badly. What would his future hold? Wildly his imagination ran riot. No wonder. The surgeon had made it clear in no uncertain words: his leg was in a mess. Unless they amputated this weekend, gangrene would set in.

Not *my* leg, thought Bob. Over my dead body! He wanted BOTH legs and to be able to *use* them! Surely the God of the universe, He who was interested in sparrows, would lend ear to him and heed his earnest longing to keep both his legs.

Sister was short and firm that night before going off duty. She tapped Bob's shoulder assuring him that there was no hope for his leg and unless he agreed to the amputation, there would be no hope for him.

Bob lay grim-faced but determined . . . until a young night nurse greeted him cheerfully. He'd not much to say, and nurse, not finding his treatment chart, did what she could to make him comfortable for the night.

It was then she smelled the wound and determinedly investigated it. Having assessed the situation, her night became *THE* night of commitment: every half hour, interrupting her other work, she cleaned the furiously pussing wound and dressed it gently.

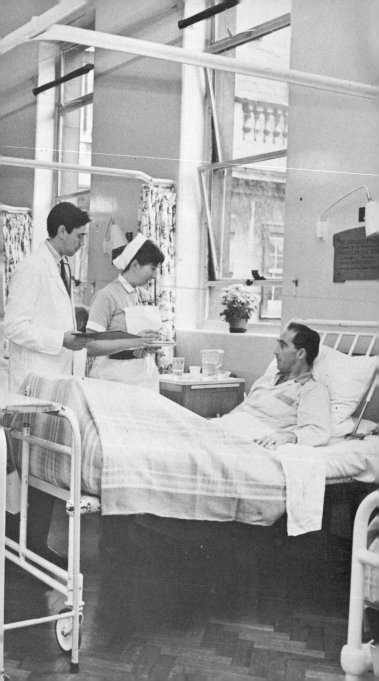

By morning, Bob was a different being. The fever had left him, so had the nurse, but his future had changed radically.

When the surgeon did his rounds that day, Bob smiled, awaiting his decision. He wasn't wrong, the Chief nodded his head: 'Bob, you've won, see you again next week, you're through, you're on the mend.'

This happened fifty years ago.

Bob's not only got his legs, he's also got a house, a simple but beautiful house at the seaside.

The service-plus during that dreadful night had changed the course of his life.

Today Bob still lives with this 'plus' which the young nurse had left him as a legacy. She herself died from influenza, but her 'plus' is shared out by Bob each day of his life.

I sampled it today!

John 10:10–11

29 Know your Employee

He needed a plug, a 13 amp., and hesitantly stood in front of the shop window gazing down at the display in front of him.

Winter had come so suddenly, he'd promised to fix the plug to that new fire by evening . . . yet couldn't bring himself to enter the premises he'd faced for the past three minutes.

An almost unchanging repertoire would undoubtedly *have* to be faced.

Last week he had listened to it, free of charge, with his regular gallon of paraffin. He had just listened and now and then shook his head in dismay or acknowledgement of sympathy.

'They think you're superhuman,' she'd rattled on, 'you come here on time each morning, but heating? No, no provision for that! Too dangerous, my foot! she's too mean, that's what she is. She tells me to keep moving, that'll keep me warm, she says! And the mess behind the counter each morning, as if she couldn't have sorted this and put it on the shelves herself before she left last night! I can't do everything! Always interruptions, customers in and out, how can anyone get straightened out before she comes in at ten o'clock?

'Her husband isn't much better, but he stays clear of me!'

He wondered 'why', as he slowly walked to the bus stop to catch a 181 to another shop—for that 13 amp. plug.

He, too, would have been an unwelcome interruption as she attempted to clear *that* muddle behind *that* counter!

James 2:2, 8–9

30 The Steak Pie's Off

Why didn't he accept the fact? Surely it wasn't *her* fault. He wasn't at a banquet . . . a holiday . . . just sailing down the Clyde! He wouldn't have starved without his favourite, just for this one day!

The steamer's first sitting for dinner had passed without any unpleasant incidents. Margaret thoroughly enjoyed her new job as waitress on the ship, but this last customer at the second sitting had come prepared for trouble!

Steak pie is what he wanted!

Steak pie it had to be!

Margaret received permission to offer him fresh salmon, ham salad, the best! It took the head waiter to convince Mr Sourface that it was impossible to give him what he wanted. He was late and the steak pie was off!

Disgruntled, he settled for fried fish.
Margaret's routine continued. The memory of Mr Sourface haunted her for the rest of the season. How many like him would she have to deal with?

Yet Margaret had chosen this summer job because she *liked* people and wanted to serve them!

Margaret wanted to give, *she* did!

Mr Sourface wanted to give, *he* did!

To-day I met Margaret, she cheered *my* day.

She gave!

Acts 8:22–23

31 Autumn

Dear Kirsty,

Of course I will try to write to you about autumn. You tell me you like the trees and all the colour of the leaves, green, orange and red. When they fall off, on chilly evenings, you love to stroll among them, your feet playing chasing games, as the leaves flutter before you with each step.

Well, I don't like *chilly* evenings, you know that quite well, but I remember when last we met in autumn and the nights were still quite light and the evening sun brought such a warm glow over all the land and our trees.

I watched them as we strolled along towards the Home Farm. Whenever an extra strong breeze blew through our hair, it also caught hold of those branches above us, and gently ruffled them back and forth, whispering: 'let go—let go—let go!' And so, the leaves came down . . . over us, on us and before our feet. Remember how gently they were severed from the branches and how equally gently they came to us to make us glad . . . and how we loved it all!

You know Kirsty, while I write to you, I *think* of those trees who parted with their lovely leaves just . . . to cheer us and make us full of wonder.

22-5-73

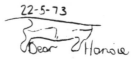

Dear Hansie

Please could you
write a story about the Autumn.
For instance when the trees look
lovely with colours of orange, red
green yellow. And lovely chilly evenings.
And you just need to kick the
leaves to keep cheery when your
finishing your walk Please could
you try and do it

love
from
KIRSTY
X ⌣ Y⌣

To HANSIE
from KIRSTY

And these big strong trees are like big strong and loving Mummies and Daddies. The little buds are born in spring and later we see them grow into juicy green leaves. People begin to admire those wonderful crowns of leaves high above, but it is really the tree itself who grew them and gave them to us. He held them tight and fed them until they were big and strong enough to be beauty to all.

But . . . people could only *look* at them, not *use* them and play with them.

And so, the leaves changed and changed and changed. And the children grew and grew and grew until the time came and life gently told branches and leaves 'come on, come on, please share yourselves with others. You have been together for so long, now please come and play with others. Please come and be our friends!'

And the leaves fluttered away and came down to us, Kirsty. Children too flutter, not only with friends in the garden, but they flutter to other gardens and other fields and other homes, and like the leaves, wherever they go they bring happiness to others.

And we love our autumn, we love our trees,

and we love all the children,

who give, like

those leaves.

Matthew 18:1–5   Revelation 22:2

32 The Cow

She's been busy for hours . . . eating!

And there she lies . . . relaxing at last! Chewing, chewing, chewing!

That's life!

Does she wonder just *why* she is here? Can a vet convince us that she

contemplates her existence?

She's a cow!

Nevertheless she gives! Milk, butter, cheese and last of all, she gives

her beef!

How peaceful her walk, how unruffled her days, yet how valuable a life for each one of us.

Don't we all want to *be* the best we can,

Don't we all want to give of our best,

Don't we all get frustrated so very often . . .

We don't *see* the result of our existence!

Neither does the cow!

She eats and chews and all other functions fall into line.

We will be productive if . . . we 'eat' the Word of God and chew it over and over again, then relax in communion with Him, whose company adds 'the spices' to the food we have eaten . . . His Holy Spirit gives LIFE to His Word, and . . .

all other functions also fall into line . . .

for us.

John 15:1–14

33 Her Sister,

in every respect as charming and generous, was having a very tough time in a byre fifty yards down the road.

As nature would have it, a fine calf was about to be born!

It should have come as easy as milk, and naturally too

but . . . it did not! She had to admit defeat!

The first time in her life, she just could not . . . give!

Her plight was noticed by one, then another, who called in a third . . . the vet! None could help her by getting to the bottom of the trouble, 'the trouble' would not move! The life within her was just flickering, but hopes were high. The men worked feverishly to shift the calf to bring it where it belonged . . .

into life!

She-lived-to-give-but-could-not!

92

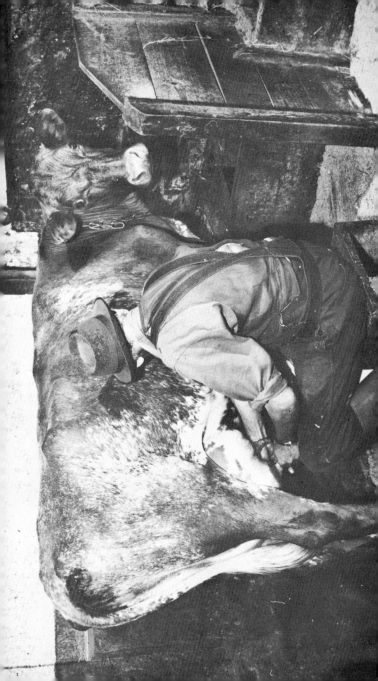

Help came from all quarters to aid her and accomplish what she knew must be!

Too late! The life within her died!

Inside our skin there, too, is life. This living soul needs care and love and oft along life's awkward road come those who long to shift the load . . . those who know . . .

this soul must live!

★   ★   ★

They work and watch and pray and aim, to see it enter . . . into

LIFE!

2 Corinthians 4:16–18, 5:1

34 September

Yes, in September, you can see her high above the golden earth from which the corn is redeemed. On the huge mountainous stacks of corn she stands serene, while the lorry moves on and on, accepting load after load.

Her face just radiates the inner qualities that stir within this one woman among all those hard-working men.

How can one define what is visible in just this fleeting glance which arrests the attention, and makes the onlooker drink in this whole picture, storing the scene in his memory? Such justifiable pride, as she scans the acres. Such gratitude for the miracle of creation, the miracle of this produce. The thrill of being part of this miracle! Such joy from somewhere deep within her! Yes, that's what's radiating from this young and sun-tanned face: joy and gratitude.

This was her picture in September. Every month of the year you will find her in another setting. Each month brings its own responsibilities for a farmer's wife. Her days begin well before six and stretch frequently into the early hours of the next: but wherever she is and whatever the time of day, every ounce of strength and each new breath influences for good all those whose lives touch hers.

The beauty, purity and strength of another sphere,

has cast its rays . . . on us.

Matthew 5:16

35 Janie and David

Yes, fancy that, the height of nonsense, just two feet-four, light as an arrow and swift as a bow. And David? He just topped these vital statistics but just . . . and no more!

This delightful, cheerful, handsome twosome was a daily sight and still is, at the bottom of the Avenue! But they've grown since first they got together.

Did they *ever* begin?

When did one not see them? Sun, wind, rain or snow, this cheerful twosome raced along. One day 'twas Janie, the next it was Dave, nothing and no one upsetting their pace.

Their errand—the paper, the daily news,

'it had to be early at the old folk's house.'

Their errand: a pattern, inbred into both,

by father and mother, to serve always those

who are nearest at hand and will only rely,

on uncomplicated deeds by this

cheerful small fry!

97

To serve, comes so easy to those thus trained

in the footsteps of Him who knew

what would be gained . . .

for everyone benefits from simple acts like these!

We who observe are blessed on the way;

and granny and grandpa enjoy their new day . . .

while Janie and David will one day recall,

'Mum and Dad gave to us of their all.'

Love and discipline, those happy rails,

running our life thus . . . to the end of our days!

Proverbs 1:7–9

36 Can't You See?

He drove a hearse, it created a stir, he loved to be seen with that 'thing'. It wasn't expensive, but useful it was and look at the space there is in it!

'Boy what a super thing, should have had this before . . .' so, Harry drove round and about.

His parents were speechless over that 'thing'—a doctor and nurse with a hearse in their drive—how could their own son fall for that? He first grew a beard, then side-locks, long hair . . . and his clothes showed the glimpse of despair!

Now a hearse!

Can't you see, can't you see, I resort to a hearse, it's all I can hope for in life. You don't know me, you don't, you never once tried, you are proud of my brother, he reached for the sky. His job as a pilot brought status to you; tin-god and a by-word his name. Willie has no problems, Willie has a vision . . . and mine became blurred even more.

Blurred, nearly blind . . . as this tin-god, so perfect, bruised our family unit . . .

It bruised—and broke—and bled!

There's a flicker of life still left here within, a flicker, a flicker, you hear? Can't you see, can't you see, I have covered it well, with long hair and side-locks and gear. And lower down I'm wearing those beads, there where *your* stethoscope hangs. Quietly you listen to many a heart, during the course of your day. Mine too is beating, mine too has a throb, but you are so busy . . . so busy.

Willie is high and I am so low and never the twain shall meet. He flies a plane and I ride a hearse and a hearse I will ride again.

Can't you see, can't you see, I too need your love, but I'm no Willie, I'm me. I shall drive my old hearse till I drive it no more; till someone will drive it for me . . . then I will meet the Great One, whose span of knowledge reaches

EVERYONE!

Can't you see, can't you see . . . I now have a Father who *EVEN* loves ME!

1 Samuel 16:7b

37 Wake Up

Like David and Jonathan; like Ruth and Naomi; yes, that's the only way he could describe their friendship. Both were happily married, but at times it needed a man to understand a man's problems and perplexities.

They'd shared them together, at all times. Hawkeye would have called them blood-brothers. Well, he wasn't far wrong. They *were* like brothers.

It is years now since the relationship came to an abrupt end, as only death can do.

To-day he walks as in a dream, attends to his business as an inevitable must, eats, sleeps and lives well, just because he still happens to be alive.

This is Remembrance Sunday.

One thinks of the many who sacrificed their lives that we might live. The many who lost sight or were maimed and will never be able to live normal lives . . . as he can . . . but he doesn't think!

He only pines for *his* friend, *his* Jonathan!

Awake, you, cocooned in misty sorrow! Awake!

Thousands are looking for a person just like you!

BE a Jonathan!

38 Butcher, Baker and Candlestick Maker

Only the butcher is left. The bread now is mass produced, we don't know all those bakers throughout the city and we surely don't know a single candlestick maker.

But I like my butcher! He's always got a civil word for me. He knows me by name and he knows that on Thursdays it is sausages and chips. He will never embarrass me with chops so late in the week. Yes, I like my butcher!

I like the crew of the Cleansing Department. They are here once a week, like clockwork. However heavy that bin, they'll remove it, and leave everything spotless to begin another week.

They smile when they come up the path and they nod politely when they leave. Yes, I like that crew!

I also like the paper boy. He leaves our breakfast luxury in the letter-box long before we rise. He never fails. Never! Come wind, storm, rain—Bill is there to entertain! Yes, that's how he does his job: as if he's there to entertain!

There's the milkman and his fetch-and-carry boys; the street sweepers; the postman; the cobbler at the corner; the ticket collector at the station; the neighbour who stops to offer a lift; the church officer who works more than his quota; the slater who comes after hours—for he won't see me stuck during the night with a leaking roof; the electrician who will do an extra job and won't accept a penny; the small shopkeeper who will leave his shop in the care of another to see me home because the groceries are too heavy; the little girl who offers me a chat and a drink of juice when I feel strange in the new hospital ward; and, and, and, and, oh, and all those other people who join the ones already mentioned and make it so worthwhile . . . to live!

Psalm 133:1

39 That Gang of Youths

They had but one aim; to help those who *could* do what they *couldn't*! Save lives from the sea!

A life raft! Yes, they would love to present a life raft to those who could use it! But how?

The seed of goodwill germinated within each boy and girl, each young man and young woman. It was watered each Sunday by the Word of God from the lips of His servant, and the application interpreted by the Holy Spirit as each young person was tended by Him individually.

The weeks went by, the project was discussed, the plans were made, resulting in action: they would work *hard* at any job, to earn the money for the raft.

The project was made public the following weekend by an advertisement in the local paper.

Would they be able to cope with all the replies? Had they not attempted a little too much in offering themselves so generously to any and everyone? Already their friends and parents had offered them jobs of various kinds. Had they bitten off more than they were able to chew?

'Those who honour Me, I will honour,' saith the Lord, whom you seek to serve in giving yourself to others.

The entire project was under His control.

*   *   *

One, just *one* reply was received in answer to the elaborately displayed advertisement. For the writer it was an answer to a prayer of long duration: Who would be willing to help him? *Who* would be willing? For years he had coped alone. Now the deprived one's personal life, the entire effort of just living, plus a wild garden, had overwhelmed him entirely.

Would the young people be willing to give a hand, to 'scalp' the garden, demolish what was necessary and dangerous to the passer-by and give the entire establishment a new look of neatness and dignity? He would pay well towards the raft, but *would they do it?*

*   *   *

The work developed into a delightfully-devastating day!

A fleet of cars arrived in the quiet country road, youngsters, in colourful working gear, spilling from each one. Armed with spades, rakes, shears of all sizes and description . . . they set to!

All around the house their lively chatter and laughter removed any doubt regarding their aim and the result of this 'job'.

Here, they served their Lord with gladness and singleness of heart. Here, their profession of faith expressed itself in actions of grace. Here, their prayers were answered by personal involvement . . . they finished a great job to perfection—giving themselves, without taking a penny in return.

Micah 6:6–8

40 Barbed-wire Reception

Close on twenty years she had been visiting the same hairdresser. It had been a regular outing, almost fun to spend a morning between junior shampoo girl, the artistic hair-setter and the stylist. There was always that inevitable cup of tea with a crisp digestive biscuit.

Elsa knew all her sheep, her broad grin greeted each one with warmhearted courtesy when she asked for 'The Coat'. Robed in a peach gown you reported to reception before retiring to a cosy foam armchair to await your turn.

But it was the *odd* moments *between* Elsa and the armchair which were so important, so desirable, so encouraging.

Cathy, the receptionist! Yes, that meant everything. She just *made* your day! From the time of phoning your appointment until you actually saw her, an expectancy beyond words built up. No one but *you* seemed to matter at the moment of meeting. Had she a photographic memory?

'Did you manage to save that mince after you slammed down the phone?' was her opening remark.

'Mince! What mince?' I hesitated, then recalled my terrifying shriek and the flight to the kitchen where something brown sizzled in the bottom of my new non-stick pan.

Sure I remembered; anyone other than Cathy might have termed me as definitely rude—slamming the receiver on the hook as I had done.

* * *

I have just phoned for a new appointment. Christopher Columbus! who was that on the other end? It wasn't Cathy. Where was she?

A sophisticated, affected voice informed me that Cathy had had to leave for health reasons and was working in a job nearer home. *She* would make an appointment for me. Would she? No, she *told* me *to come* at 2.30 p.m.

Not me! I took the jitters; it would need a lot of courage to go past *that* 'barbed-wire' to my well-known and much loved armchair and its successive delights.

I replaced the receiver gently on the hook. We had been cut off!

Hebrews 12:15 NEB

41 Mother

Each morning at eight o'clock, George exercised his young spaniel in the large park at the back of his home. This morning, no different from any other, he threw the ball far into the football pitch. Bruce raced to fetch it. Time was short, George had to catch the 8.45 a.m. into town.

No one had joined his early constitutionals before, but to-day a young teenager slowly entered the park gates. He recognised Allen at once. Fancy seeing him here.

Allen soon explained his mysterious appearance. He'd come to stay in the Avenue, in digs, to be nearer his work.

'In digs!' George exclaimed. 'But why? your home's only a few miles away. Nothing serious the matter? Are your parents unwell? Someone in hospital? Death?'

'Oh, no,' Allen lightheartedly began, 'nothing like that.'

He spoke for a solid ten minutes, while his land-lady's terrier and George's spaniel celebrated a new friendship.

'You knew about my occasional spells in the Psychiatric Unit of Rosevale. What you didn't know, was *the cause*! You see, it's my homelife! It worries me stiff. Father and Mother argue their heads off. Not major problems, mind you, but creepy small things, hardly worth repeating. Dad hasn't a chance, she's always right, and somehow, I can't open my mouth on any subject but she gets at me. It's no fun being at home, George. My sisters laugh their heads off, but I can't, it hits me right down to my nerves. Like surprise guerilla attacks, you know, and it gets me down.

'Away from home, I'm like a bird with outstretched wings, enjoying God's free air, the friendship of my workmates, my landlady, and her dog.'

They had to part or George would miss his train.

That night he not only carried his briefcase into the house, but also a large bunch of chrysanthemums for his stunned-faced wife.

George, too, had three teenage children and his home hadn't been all that . . . well, you know . . . lately . . . !

Would one of *his* children ever talk like Allen?

Romans 12:18–19

113

42 Winter

It is strange, but the very word 'winter' chills a person through and through, even those who wait for its arrival in order to conquer the ski slopes in the country of their choice. Even they have to 'prepare' themselves to meet the conditions which are created by this season of the year.

If not prepared in the proper manner, they'll soon experience *who* is boss, *who* is the stronger, *who* is not to be ignored.

And so, winter 'tones' us all in one way or another. He strips us of our sluggishness and creates within an alert awareness . . . to be prepared!

But 'winter', such a general word, is used for all and sundry. *You* know the person who creates an icy atmosphere. *You* know the chill which hits your heart when he suddenly enters a room. *You* know too that wintry-glistening road . . . you must often travel alone.

Yet 'winter' is an unstable word

    a general melting term,

for its cold and its ice wherever found

    will eventually cause concern.

You discover it was but a passing phase . . .

for mountains still cradled in their misty shroud,

change completely when the sun

           breaks out

    as grace into the heart.

Winter is never a permanent state,

    the cycle so well designed

        hides firm underneath those frosty paths

    the miracle . . .

        of snowdrops!

John 11 : 25, 43   1 Samuel 16 : 7b

43 Calder Street

Those gusts of wind meeting her at every corner made it nigh impossible to carry that 4′ × 3′ sheet of plywood to the bus stop just some ten minutes from the store.

She'd been planning all the way along: wouldn't it be great to have this hanging over her child's bed when she returned from school? A smile lit up her tired face as she realised that in no time the board would be covered with pin-ups of today's pop stars, postcards, a calendar and the school's timetable.

If only the store manager hadn't been so short-tempered that morning. It had been so early in the day and he hadn't even opened the shop properly. . . . She hadn't had the heart to ask for wrapping or string to transport this large monstrosity home.

Only one hand available, and an injured one at that. The other, damaged in the same accident, held on tightly to her handbag, tools and yet another smaller piece of wood.

Every five to ten steps she slipped it gently down to her shoe, allowing the hand to clench and un-clench . . . it could almost hold no longer. She simply *had* to get home! Would the bus conductor allow her on the platform with such a thing?

Someone passed her, then retraced their steps. Furrows along her forehead, curlers in her hair—partly covered by a slightly faded head scarf—her work-a-day coat hanging loosely over stockings which concertina'ed merrily around her vein-marked legs, fitting into shoes which were worse of wear . . . there stood a LADY!

'Come on luv,' she exclaimed, concernedly, 'I'll gie ye a wee haun alang the road. Whaur are ye goin'?'

Tears popped into the eyes of our human-donkey. Swallowing hard, she could only answer: 'To the bus'.

And into the bus she was pushed by . . . a LADY.

Psalm 90:17

44 Eighty-Five Today!

His house and his goods and time were his own.

He's free, no ties and no one to tell; all of his ways can be chosen well.

He comes and goes, he's in, then out; his car tops 40000, it's a simple life.

Two world wars he's seen, wisdom pours from these lips . . .

In dress, speech and manner, describe a gentleman . . . it fits!

Never before have I met such a gracious man, such a humble and happy extraordinary

man.

He washes and irons, he gardens and cleans, he writes and he reads and he sows many seeds. With alert intelligence judging competitions, as photographic expert

making rightful decisions.

He trains and teaches at home and elsewhere, all who wish to discuss how

to love and care.

His textbook since youth

the Bible, just that,

hence his life is poured out for the other chap.

His time and his house, his talents, his all, have always belonged to the

Source of his call.

★   ★   ★

This Source, his Sustenance,

his aim, his delight,

owing all . . . he *is* owned . . .

yet a free man for LIFE!

John 8:32, 36   John 15:16

Photo: Copyright Douglas Scott ▶

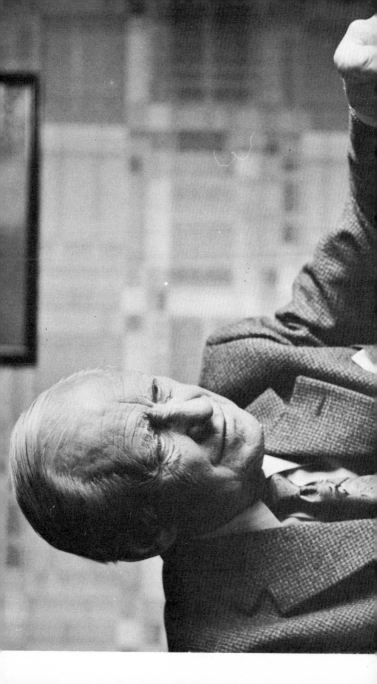

45 Coincidental Nonsense

No order nor plan in all our lives, just a jumble of chancy events. Everyone wants to know *why* this-or-that 'just happens'.

I didn't fly in that plane last week,

he *just happened* to meet that guy.

And guess what he found in his pocket to-day

when he thought his kitty was dry!

Yesterday morn my car broke down . . .

the A.A. came round the bend,

but the second time it came to a halt . . .

outside a mechanic's tent.

Then on I travelled for many more miles . . .

until finally I *reached* home,

and *there* I was told the cause of all this:

I needed a dynamo.

Tragedy or joyful events

I wouldn't ascribe it to chance

Let's seek to know

just Who's in control . . .

and falt'ringly our trust will grow, that really
Somebody cares!

Until we reach 'the other side'

Let's admit it *can* look a mess

But *then* we'll see even as we are seen, and no
longer we'll be left . . .

to guess!

Job 22:12–14   John 16:7, 22–24

46 God so loved, that He gave . . .
John 3:16

There will be few who have not heard 'that story' at some time or another. One has become so accustomed to the words that all meaning seems to have been boiled out, as from a knap-bone which no longer produces stock!

Allow yourself to be tanned by the warmth and reality that,

nevertheless . . . it is so!

The *in*visible Godhead gave

the visible Christ to the world and

His *in*visible Spirit is available for you.

God is a Spirit, and they that worship Him, must worship Him in spirit and in truth.

Each visit to a crematorium or open graveside,

every undertaker's office,

makes us aware that *we* are spirit.

125

Once our spirit is willing to be lit by its Origin

to blaze within,

its life will affect the container

our body!

Then we, too, may continue to carry the Olympic
Torch, lit within a human container

in Bethlehem.

His purpose . . . to *give* eternal Life . . .
abundantly.

We live . . . to give . . .

WHAT?

John 17:18